GOD
IS NOT
SANTA
DOING AWAY WITH THE WISH LISTS

AARON RYAN

Award-winning author of the bestselling alien invasion series
Dissonance, the bestselling Christian post-apocalyptic series
The End, the 9/11 historical fiction thriller *Forecast*, and *The Christian Kids Values, Identity & Affirmation* Picture Book Series

Published in 2025, Edition 1.

Paperback ISBN # 9781965372326 · Hardcover ISBN #
9781965372333 · eBook ISBN # 9781965372319.

Edited by CM LLC. Published independently.

Cover art by CM LLC.

This is a work of nonfiction. Any similarities to persons living
or dead, or actual events is purely coincidental.

For Sweeps, Bren & AJ:
my true loves.

Thank you for being the very fulfillment
of my Wish List.

Chapters

*"Prayer does not change God,
but it changes him who prays."*

- Søren Kierkegaard

Note on A.I.

We live in an age of AI. Every day, more and more services spring up promising revolutionary and innovative results using artificial intelligence. The authoring industry is not immune to this.

I want every one of my readers to know that not once did I employ, nor will I *ever* employ, the use of AI to sculpt any part of any of my stories. Those who know me know that I am staunchly and adamantly opposed to such cheats.

I'm very proud to be a verified human. The ability to create is a gift that I was endowed by my Creator, and I will never forfeit that nor set it aside to propagate something synthetic and imitative.

Everything you've read by me in this saga, and in all my other works, is 100% entirely created by me, the genuine article. I'm a verified human, and always will be.

To my fellow authors, I urge you to preserve the sacred gift of human creation and never stoop to such lows. Always cherish this gift you've been given. If you encounter writer's block, take a break. Don't cop out. Don't take the road more traveled by. Don't cheat. Toe the line for all of us, and keep creation – *true* unadulterated creation – alive.

Long live humanity.

Sincerely,

Aaron Ryan,
Verified Human

Chapter 1: Gratitude

"Gratitude is the fairest blossom which springs from the soul."

-Henry Ward Beecher

An "attitude of gratitude." We've all heard it. The number one thing beyond anything else, and the foundation for being successful in life…or in anything?

An attitude of gratitude.

I'm a voiceover artist and an author. If you were a fly on the wall in my office, every time I'm awarded a job or receive a notification that I've sold a book, you will hear me say, "Thank You, Lord." I will say that literally every single time.

Every time some client writes back and says, "Thank you for sending your demo," or "Yes, we'd love to put you on our roster" or "I loved your book" or even "I wasn't too keen on this book, but I did buy it": Once again, *thank you, Lord.*

An attitude of gratitude. Whomever you want to thank is entirely up to you. But that attitude of gratitude lays the foundation for future success.

Always be grateful. Always proceed in gratitude. Never forget the first client who hired you. Never forget to say thank you to the workers in the drive-thru, though they barely say thank you anymore for patronizing their establishment. It's become a bit of an epidemic, this loss of gratitude and this basic lack of manners. It's up to you and me to toe the line and stem the tide.

You can't force someone to be grateful or say thank you. Indeed, I have a 9 year old and a 6 year old son, and I can't do that with them either. It's impossible. What I can do, however, is set the example anytime I'm out in public with them, exhorting them to always employ manners and use their 'please' and 'thank you.' Both reflect gratitude for the gift given.

Many times I'll go back to my very first voiceover client ever, and I'll fire off an out-of-the-blue email such as, "Hey, I know that you're probably not thinking about me, but I was just thinking about you and wanted to say *thank you again for choosing me.*"

An out-of-the-blue email like that just shows such resounding residual gratitude that just doesn't stop. Clients are very grateful for your gratitude. *People* are grateful for a grateful attitude. So, always be grateful. Gratitude is the wheels that make the world go round.

When I was just out of high school, my well-to-do uncle, a lawyer, offered me a cash gift to help toward college. It came with one condition.

"Just don't over-thank me."

I've thought about that over the years, and my dad and I often joke about that phrase anytime we do something nice for each other. It's become a humorous byline, but I have to think back to Uncle Darrell, and wonder what he was actually saying.

Had he been over-thanked by people? Was that something that I was notorious for? Was it a problem he observed with society?

If any of those were true, we've drifted dangerously from resounding gratitude. Instead, we've traveled to the other pole. The one where we simply *expect*, and we're ungrateful. The one where we take things for granted, and we have become conditioned to simply trust that we'll always get *what* we want, *when* we want it.

I think one of the most sinister and unhelpful inventions ever made was the microwave. (The toaster is right behind it.) Talk about a device to sap our gratitude and make us *expect!* Now, before you go calling me old-fashioned, consider the example posed by comedian Brian Regan, that of cooking pop-tarts in your microwave:

Man, if you need to zap-fry your pop-tarts before you head out for the morning, you might wanna loosen up your schedule!

And, he's right. We are so accustomed to getting what we want, when we want it in this Microwave Society, and anytime we have to wait longer than three seconds, it's unbearable. In short, we're spoiled.

In short, we're ungrateful.

One of the greatest things that I am intent and diligent about teaching my children, is the attitude of gratitude. A phrase I find myself continually employing with my older son in particular is, "Be grateful for what you *do* have; not angry about what you don't."

As an author, I was able to use that phrase in the sequel to my alien invasion series, *Dissonance Volume IV: Relentless,* as voiced from the President to his wife. I find that phrase is incredibly helpful with Brennan in particular, and it's one that helps to recenter him.

Gratitude is the key to happy living. When we come to simply expect that we will receive, it's one of the most caustic and toxic places we can be. We are spoiled and expectant, petulant children that whine when we don't get our way.

Writing that paragraph, I'm suddenly propelled back in time to my childhood. I'm sitting in the living room of our North Bend Washington home, and I'm flipping through the Sears catalog and circling things that I want for Christmas. Things that I crave and wish with everything in me that I could have, with zero regard for my parents' finances, zero regard for needs versus wants, zero regard for what having yet another possession will not even bring me. *Lots* of things.

Yet, ritualistically, this is something I do every single year, expectantly, waiting to be showered with *things*. Things from my *Wish List* that I desperately wished I could have.

When I started dating my wife in 2011, I was utterly unprepared for the generosity of her father. His love language is giving. (I know someone else whose love language is giving, FYI. His name is Jesus Christ.) Janine's father, John, is an amazing man who just delights in giving good gifts to his children.

I wasn't ready to be so inundated in Christmas of 2011 with their family. I had never experienced such bounty showered upon me. The truth of the matter is that I had already received his blessing and proposed to his daughter in June of that year. He and his wife welcomed me in with open arms. John deemed me a gift to his daughter (I know: *crazy!*), and he was ready to give back to me in thanks. That first Christmas with the Wilson family blew me away.

However, in that same time period I was exposed to something I had never been aware existed. *Amazon Wish Lists*. Most of his kids, both biological and in-law, maintained such a thing. I just hadn't been privy to its existence. Well, it was an eye-opener, indeed. It was something that you could share with people and tell them *precisely* what you wanted. No more gross fruitcakes. No more erroneous sizes of shirts. No more unwanted gifts.

Exactly what I wanted. I mean, how much better does it get, right?

Sad.

A few years of this, and I couldn't stomach it any more. I gave up providing information on "what I would like" for my birthday or Christmas. I felt it was far too narcissistic and demanding for my tastes, and I abandoned it. I just didn't want to prescribe my own gifts for people.

I wanted to be surprised! I wanted to be delighted and amazed! I wanted to not know what was behind that wrapping paper and that box! To be fair, the default gift then became an Amazon gift card – ha! Or a Subway gift card. Or some variant of some gift card to somewhere that they knew that I liked. *Fine,* I thought, and I relented. I always appreciate those gift cards, but I'll be darned if I was going to give someone a recipe for my own happiness. I could be happy just receiving *time* with them. And God has given our family so much, that I truly felt, 'I don't really need anything.' I had reached a place in my life where I just didn't 'need' things, nor did I want to ask for them.

Anything received from that point forward was an unexpected delight; a surprise gift; a truly unprescribed joy. But - they always paled compared to the joy I took in giving gifts to others. I *LOVE* wrapping Christmas and birthday gifts. I truly love seeing them accumulate under the tree and know – with increasing anticipation – that eventually my sons or my wife are going to open that gift and be equally surprised by unexpected delight. They have their expressed wants, yes, but I rarely buy those. They know not to voice them, ha! Usually I'll just end up buying something else. And I never give cash gifts at Christmastime. How impersonal is that? I much prefer to give something that I know will bless someone in a way that they did not expect.

It is the unexpected that leaves us surprised by blessing.

So, let us do away with the Wish Lists and be grateful.

I ask you, should we be more concerned with receiving *things*, or with *The Thing* from which gifts come? Should we be more obsessed with gifts? Or with The Giver Himself? (NOTE: I am certainly not talking about Santa Claus here, hence the title of this book.)

As a parent of two young boys, I have my finger on the pulse of the stress of our house, sagging under the weight of 'things.' We have far too much for my liking, and if I could add a little feng shui to our home, I certainly would, vis a vis a gigantic *Everything Must Go* sale. My kids would howl in protest for years to come, and it would be music to my ears.

Toys litter the play area. Too much furniture encroaches on space. Too many clothes burgeon our closets. Far too many bikes and riding things dot our yard. Needless waste.

Is life about the accumulation of wealth? About how much you have and how much you've acquired? Or is it about something greater?

Be grateful for what you do have, not angry about what you don't.

When we take the time to breathe, to realize that there are so many in this world that do *not* have what we have, it helps us to step back, take the 10,000-foot view, and see the suffering all around us, though we had blocked it out in our foolish expectation and our consumed-with-self tunnel vision.

We are *so* consumed, as consumers in this consuming society, with consumption. It's what Agent Smith told Morpheus in *The Matrix:*

I'd like to share a revelation during my time here. It came to me when I tried to classify your species. I realized that you're not actually mammals. Every mammal on this planet instinctively develops a natural equilibrium with the surrounding environment but you humans do not. You move to an area and you multiply and multiply until every natural resource is consumed. The only way you can survive is to spread to another area. There is another organism on this planet that follows the same pattern. Do you know what it is? A virus. Human beings are a disease, a cancer of this planet. You are a plague, and we are the cure.

Yikes! Lord, save us from the Agent Smiths out there. May it not come to that. The point being, we are natural consumers, and not natural givers. We are *take-take-take*, and not *give-give-give*. God bless those for whom the natural inclination is to give; those who truly inhabit the morale behind the phrase "it is more blessed to give than to receive."

Jesus Himself, in one of the most memorable phrases he ever uttered, said "Greater Love has no one than this; that a man lay down his life for his friends." (John 15:13).

There is no Greater Love than to give. But we've got it backward (as we do with most things). We've put the cart before the horse with this, as with so many other principles in life. We consider it better to receive, to amass, to acquire and to obtain, than to relinquish, give up, donate, provide. We chase the dopamine feel-good hit of getting things. But I'd like to submit to you that you can receive the same hit in giving. Perhaps even a bigger hit.

I really appreciate – and envy – the people who are able to live a life unencumbered by *things* – and they've been able to strip down their living to only things that they *need*. I'll talk about this more in a later chapter, but ultimately those brave souls who are able to live a simpler life and rely on less material possessions...they nothing short of amaze me. I have not been able to obtain a life like that.

In so many ways, I *need* my iPhone. I *need* my Apple watch. I *need* my big-screen TV. I *need* multiple cars. I *need* a fridge in the kitchen *and* the garage. We *need* backups of backups of things. It's the "Just In Case Inventory." Because, God forbid something we have should break, and we should have to go without? GO WITHOUT?!?!? What century is this? GO WITHOUT?!?!? Are we living in the Dark Ages here?

I think what would be truly beneficial for so many people is to have to sit in the DMV on a busy Saturday when there are so many people there, waiting, waiting, waiting for their turn in line so they can *just* get on with their day. We've become impatient, us humans. Why can't we just walk in and be #1 in line? Is that too much to ask? I mean, really.

I'd like to share this poem with you that I wrote in the late nineties. It's called, quite simply, "Patience."

Patience: an inestimable element
Heavily needed, lightly given
An element forged in fire and in fire tried
Consisting in plenty during peace
And found wanting during war

Dichotomy? Indeed
Encouraged by old, wrinkled men
Who couldn't wait to get to wisdom
Counted blessed by encouraging mothers
And screamed for by the same

Lifted high on virtuous flag waving
In gusts that battle their way back to the sea
Borne slowly then upon rolling tide
Which returns to barrage age-strong shores
Strange…

I can't wait to have patience…

I can't wait to have patience. In my impatience, I lose gratitude. Instead of being grateful about what I *do* have (four limbs, the ability to breathe, a working phone, a family to return home to), I can become angry about what I don't have (time, ability to do certain other activities, lack of freedom to obtain a different environment).

I create my own prison when I behave this way, expecting things to be exactly as I ordain, and not being grateful to simply *sit* and simply *be.* Psalm 46:10 urges me to "be still and know that [He is] God." We have that verse in artwork set above our living room fireplace, for goodness' sake. Ya know, it's right there: perched right above our TV, which we use to drown out… *Psalm 46:10.*

Dichotomies everywhere.

It is *utterly* critical for us as human beings to be grateful. Here's the million-dollar lesson:

Gratitude comes not from having, but from giving.

Now, that part is about the gift. With that part out of the way, let us now focus on some giving.

Chapter 2: Giving

"We make a living by what we get, but we make a life by what we give."

-Winston Churchill

Shel Silverstein. Ring a bell? That name ought to conjure up some incredibly rich memories for anyone growing up in the 70's or 80's. Shel was the inimitable author of such fantastic stories as *A Light in the Attic, The Missing Piece, Falling Up, Runny Babbit, Every Thing On It, a Giraffe and a Half, Where The Sidewalk Ends,* and many more.

One particular story holds immeasurable weight for my boys, particularly at bedtime and story time It's called *The Giving Tree*, and it's utterly beautiful.

The Giving Tree tells the story of a tree that loves a little boy so much that it offers everything to that boy. It invites the boy to climb up into its branches, to eat its fruit, to enjoy its shade. Over time, the boy grows older, falls in love with someone else, develops a career and a family, and ages. Repeatedly, the tree gently encourages the boy – who he always calls 'boy' despite his age, indicating the cherished memory that the tree is holding onto – to take advantage of itself. Whether that's through sitting in its shade and taking a load off, cutting down its branches or sawing it down to the trunk to build a boat or a house, the tree utterly expends itself for the boy…because it loves him so much. The boy marches onward with life, but frequently returns to that tree. Though too old now to climb branches and pick fruit, too tired to play, and too careworn to be as much in love with the tree as the tree is in love with him, he returns yet again.

Finally, the tree is so removed from its former glory that it has little else to offer the boy except for a stump for the boy to sit on and rest. And that is truly enough for the boy in the story, as he dabs his sweat away. Just to rest. The tree itself is so proud and moved and *grateful* – there's that buzz word again! – to be able to provide something –

anything for the boy. All it longs to do is to provide. To give.

And that's where the story ends. The tree has been reduced to a small, flat stump, while the old man rests upon it. It has given everything to provide for his comfort and his happiness.

The only part of that story where I wish Silverstein had gone a bit further would be to have had that tree offer itself to be the old man's *coffin*. It literally would have expended itself *utterly,* and it would have died along with its beloved boy, wrapping its wood and its roots around him for all eternity, cradling him in love, having given everything to form his sarcophagus. That would be the quintessential gift and would have provided, in my humble opinion, an even more powerful ending. Nonetheless, it's plenty powerful as it stands, and the story illustrates how much someone is willing to give, how far someone is willing to go, to ensure that you have what you need.

A loving parent is no less a giver. There's the story of the hen and her chicks, as recounted by Wayne Jacobsen. Regardless of whether this account is true or not (it's debated)[1], it remains highly inspirational.

The forest fire had been brought under control, and the group of firefighters were working back through the devastation making sure all the hot spots had been extinguished. As they marched across the blackened landscape between the wisps of smoke still rising from the smoldering remains, a large lump on the trail caught a firefighter's eye.

As he got closer he noticed it was the charred remains of a large bird, that had burned nearly half way through. Since birds can so easily fly away from the approaching flames, the firefighter wondered what must have been wrong with this bird that it could not escape. Had it been sick or injured?

Arriving at the carcass, he decided to kick it off the trail with his boot. As soon as he did, however, he was startled half to death by a flurry of activity around his feet. Four little birds flailed in the dust and ash then scurried away down the hillside.

The bulk of the mother's body had covered them from the searing flames. Though the heat was enough to consume her, it allowed her babies to find safety underneath. In the face of the rising flames, she had stayed with her young. She was their only hope for safety, and willing to risk her own life she gathered them under her body and covered them with herself. Even when the pain reached its most unbearable moment, when she could easily have flown

away to start another family on another day, she made
herself stay through the raging flames.

Her dead carcass and her fleeing chicks told the story well
enough—she gave the ultimate sacrifice to save her
young. It also illustrates an even greater story—this one
almost incomprehensible. In this story it is the Creator of
heaven and earth who does exactly the same thing to
rescue his wayward children from their own destruction.[2]

Isn't that incredible? A mother hen burned to death
protecting her chicks from the fire. Kind of reminds you of
someone else who died to protect us from the fire, no?
*checks notes** Oh, that's right! I'm talking about Jesus.

Speaking of fire, I remain moved to this day by the bravery,
heroism, and selfless sacrifice displayed by those brave
343 firefighters who rushed in to protect the people
trapped in the World Trade Center towers on September
11th, 2001. I remain moved to this day by the bravery,
heroism, and selfless sacrifice displayed by those thirty-
five to forty passengers and crew who rushed the cockpit
in a valiant attempt to retake flight United 93 that ended up
crashing in Shanksville, Pennsylvania.

On that day so many years ago, extremists hijacked four
United States passenger aircraft[3] and drove them into
oblivion, in order to kill as many Americans as possible.

We call it 9/11.

Now, I am no expert on religious fanaticism, and I am very
often loth to venture into any form of political realm
whatsoever, but I ask you to put your political leanings and
conspiracy theories aside for just a moment, restore your
seat back to its full upright position, and remember with
me.
I am going to talk about those whose voices were forever
lost.

I am sure, like most people, we all know where we were
during the following:

- When JFK was assassinated[4]
- When man landed on the moon[5]
- When Challenger exploded[6]
- When Reagan was shot[7]
- When Princess Diana died[8]
- September 11th, 2001[9]
- When Michael Jackson died[10]
- When Columbine[11], Parkland[12], Sandy Hook[13],
  Uvalde[14] and so many others happened

If you are like me, then your world stopped. I know you
remember the days clearly as I do. I wasn't alive for JFK
or when man landed on the moon, but I remember the

others clearly. As a parent, my heart stopped the hardest on the days of those horrible school shootings, especially Uvalde. In the days following, I remember watching my kids board their bus and literally asking myself, with a lump in my throat, "Did I just send them off to school....or to *eternity?*" Tragic.

I remember precisely where I was on September 11th, and I will remember it until I am old and grey. It is something that I hold very tenderly and somberly in my heart as one of the worst wounds I have ever taken, and one of the worst burdens I have ever experienced weighing upon my spirit.

For the very first time on the morning of September 11th 2022, I showed my 6-year-old son footage of airplanes being deliberately flown into the World Trade Center. I wept as I told him that all the people on board American Airlines Flight 11 instantly died, as well as anyone in the North Tower who was in the impact zone.

I wept later as we saw the second plane, United Airlines Flight 175, smash into the South Tower. I wept later when the third plane, American Airlines Flight 77, disappeared like a missile into the Pentagon. I wept again, convulsively, as I showed him pictures of a giant crater in Shanksville, Pennsylvania, where the heroes and victims of United Airlines Flight 93 will forever rest. And I wept yet again as I showed him footage of the south tower, and then the north tower, collapsing.

Apparently I cry a lot.

Why did I weep? I wept because, all those years later, I am now a parent of two small children. And the thought of losing either one or both of them in such tragedy terrifies me. 9/11 was all about terror. Conversely, the thought of my children losing one or both of their parents in such tragedy terrifies me. More than 3000 children lost a parent on 9/11.[15] Eight children were killed: five on American Flight 77, and three on United Airlines Flight 175.[16]

There is solace in grief. Weeping eventually runs its course. Wells run dry. But we all need to grieve: there are heart issues when you do not grieve. In fact, Dr. Dan Allender once said, "All addiction is failure to grieve."[17] We *must* grieve, or we will not learn a thing.

So: I grieve every September 11th, and understand me when I say that it is good. I need to reflect. I need to remember the sacrifices made on that day. I never want to take for granted the world we live in, or the relative safety we currently live in here in the United States, though we are occasionally buffeted by unspeakable tragedy. In such an unsafe world, I desperately pray my children are safe.

I used to be a singer. In 2009, I partnered with a friend to create and produce a song called *Whisper.* This is a work that was near and dear to my heart because, on 9/11, I was going through a very self-absorbed and selfish time of my life, and so, the full weight of it was somewhat lost on me. However, 5 years afterwards, the full reality of it crippled me, and I authored a poem which would eventually take life in the form of this song.

It is 9 minutes and 11 seconds long. And coincidentally, it turned out to be the 11th song on my 9th collection of musical works.

It is good and healthy to reflect, and not forget. This is my song, *Whisper.*

In the audio version of the song, you hear several audio samples that are actually taken from the day itself. In the end, you hear the lonely unanswered plea from the radio tower in Cleveland trying to raise United 93. And at the very end, you will hear the haunting firefighter "PASS device"[18] – a locator beacon – that was sounding in droves from the smoldering heap of the fallen towers – attached to 343 valiant heroes whose voices would never be heard again.

We must always remember, and never forget.

(By the way, that phrase above is a lesson that we can apply to SO many areas of our life, not just remembering 9/11. We must *always* remember how good we have it…and never forget.)

The song is called *Whisper* because we need to dare to hear the *whisper* of voices that will never be heard again:

- Fathers that would never use their voices to tell a bedtime story
- Mothers that would never use their voices to sing a lullaby to their newborns
- Children whose voices would never crack and change and grow to adulthood

I remained so impacted by 9/11 that in 2024 I penned a 9/11 historical fiction novel, *Forecast*, wherein I was able to have the protagonist completely avert 9/11. In that book, it never happened. It was completely prevented. Oh, how I wish that were the truth! But it is not, and so we must go on remembering the brave sacrifice that was made for so many. As one witness observed, "all gave some, some gave all."

Here is the song:

Song of silence, teal sky
Wisps in stratus gliding by
Bastions steady guard the shore
Proud defense 'gainst woe and war

Gleam ye faintly through the night, now
Mirror sun with proud delight!
Tridents anchored, vigil landing
How you define our sense of standing

Tide of time rolls endless toward
Two twin sentinels fate ignored
Souls in progress, life ongoing
Business, schedules, comfort knowing

Meetings planned & days arranged
8:46…life is changed
Guided missile, brazen foe
Descending upon souls below

Uninclinéd victim's call
Goes unanswered in the ball
Of fire and hate and roaring noise:
Shattered ego, shaken poise

Can you hear the whisper overwhelmed by thunder

O the voices calling from the soil
Dare I feel this tremor? Will this leave me never?
Can the world be evermore the same?

Cacophony laden, bellowing gust
Seam rips silence, scattering rust
Sparks and showers, Beams and clutter
Gasping sounds of endless mutter

Wailing sirens, mirth cut short
Haunting scream of death's retort
Blackened fumes go spiraling up
Widened eyes taste anger's cup

Ever upward, steel unbending
To the point of scarréd rending
Debris aloft, splinters flying
Life and matters fall with crying

Quiet strife of woe and war has
Met most unwelcome on this shore
Were we sleeping, were we faint?
Plunging eagle, faltering saint

Tolls go meanwhile counting higher
Ebbing struggle through muck and mire
Life familiar before 8:46
What was added to the mix

Was it ego, was it might
Our chests' beat heard far through night?
Plans were hatched with venom much
Snaking through our mental clutch

Unseen foes crept through our gate
And plunged their missiles steered by hate
One stands weeping, brother down
Soon to meet him on the ground

Personal whistles sound motionless heroes
343 to 0

When I hear the sirens, fading into silence
Give me room to think and breathe and be
O to shake the sadness, to undo this madness
But the whispers haunt me to this day

Into our ribs, into our flesh
Holding ransom our precious breath
Can it be they found a way
Into our guts that vile day

O great dilemma mine!
O massive predicament mine!
How miniscule your minutiae!

Can you hear the whisper overwhelmed by thunder
O the voices calling from the soil
Dare I feel this tremor? Will this leave me never?
Can the world be evermore the same?

There is ash in my breath, breathing souls, tasting
death. Could this happen any other way?
When this night has ended, can we say we've mended
For our heroes all have sailed away

Remember. *All gave some. Some gave all.*

Remember.

We must always remember, and never forget. What do the tree in *The Giving Tree*, the hen, and the heroes of 9/11 teach us?

They teach us that giving is everything.

Receiving is nothing. Holding on to things doesn't matter. The Giving Tree gave all. The hen gave all. The heroes of 9/11 gave all. *Jesus* also gave all.

May we always remember, and never forget.

Chapter 3: Receiving

"God never gives someone a gift they are not capable of receiving. If he gives us the gift of Christmas, it is because we all have the ability to understand and receive it."

- Pope Francis

All too often we are overly consumed by receiving gifts. Growing up, I was not immune to seeing that glorious Christmas tree, and taking pains to count how many presents underneath it were mine. Both of my brothers did the same.

Both my sons now do the same. They want to see how many they're getting, as if the ratio of my love for them was somehow directly reflected by how many presents they were going to receive, or how big said presents were.

Little do my boys know or understand that the number of gifts they are to receive is incommensurate with how much their mom and I love them. One thing doesn't have anything to do with the other. We simply love them, and we give that love, and they both receive the same amount, regardless of who they were, what they had done or not done, who they had been, or who they would become.

We love them. Richly. Unreservedly. Perpetually. Freely. We give them that love, and we always will.

There's a kind of gift that this world does not understand fully: the gift that comes from the Giver Himself. The one who utterly loves to give, no matter the cost to Himself.

That Giver is God Almighty, who gave His Son, Jesus Christ, to be our redeeming sacrifice on the cross. It cost Him everything in giving up His Son. It cost His Son everything as well.

And what happened on the other end?

We received.

We received God With Us. (Immanuel, one of Jesus' Names, literally means *God With Us.*) It is the *only* recorded event in history where it was more blessed to receive than to give.

We received God in a bod! We received a kingly gift of the Most High God, wrapped in flesh, sent to save us, and to provide access to the King of the Universe! **WHAT A GIFT!**

The Bible says that we are sinners, steeped in sin from birth. John 9:34 says this. Psalm 51:5 says this. It says, "Surely I was brought forth in iniquity." Psalm 58:3 says, "Even from birth the wicked go astray." Genesis 6:5, from the beginning, says that man, *also* from the beginning, was evil, and that "every inclination of the reasonings of his heart was evil every day."

Yeeshk! What business do we have receiving such a kingly gift then?

Because of God's generosity to us. 2 Corinthians 9:67 says, "God loves a cheerful giver." I agree. And I'll wager this is true because God *Himself* is a cheerful giver. He LOVES to give! And so, He gave us His very best.

But what about receiving? Shall we expect to receive only good things, and not bad? Job 2:10 says "Should we accept from God only good and not adversity?" Certainly not. We should receive everything that the Lord hands down, with a glad and grateful heart, even though it might challenge us.

In my *Dissonance* alien invasion book series, there is a seminal character dotting the pages. Her name is Pastor Rosie. She is a diminutive Mexican septuagenarian, and she is *power-packed*. She carries wisdom like a purse, and she always has it with her. She repeatedly dispenses some bumper-sticker lessons that stick with multiple protagonists, and I loved her so much that I had her crossover into many of my other novels as well. She's *that* good! I could write an entire novel on just Rosie.

One thing that Rosie is famous for in the *Dissonance* series is 'palms up.' It's an expression – and a subsequent posture – that is taught to the remnants of mankind after the gorgon attacks, and it is so pervasive and drenched in meaning, that it carries to all the Blockades where survivors dwell. In fact, it's employed long after her death.

Quite simply, 'palms up' is all about receiving from the Lord *whatever* He wants to give you, whether good or bad.

See, Santa apparently only brings you good gifts…and that's only *if* you're good. But what about those kids who were bad? Do they really get a lump of coal in their stocking? I'd venture to say that no parent ever really does that to their children. The shame and sadness conveyed to those children would be horrifyingly unrecoverable. But good ol' St. Nicholas is renowned for bringing gifts, wrapped in sparkling wrapping paper and tied with neat little red ribbons, intended to please the hearts of every good little boy and girl, one night a year…if they're lucky.

On the contrary, God gave His Son as the greatest gift ever, to a humanity *steeped* in sin. One that could never thank Him back properly. One completely undeserving.

One that deserved lumps of coal in their stockings.

But good gifts aren't all that we receive from Him. We receive life and death. We receive blessings…and sometimes we receive much-needed discipline. Hebrews 12:6 says, "The Lord disciplines the one He loves, and he chastens everyone he accepts as His son." Why wouldn't he do that? Isn't He a loving Father?

Do I only dispense blessings to my sons? Do I give them everything they want? HECK NO. Would I spoil them in the process? Absolutely. Sometimes I give them much-needed discipline. Because, like the Lord, I love them and accept them as my sons.

Ultimately, were I to dispense everything my children wanted, I would turn them into Veruca Salt, the spoiled, bratty daughter in Roald Dahl's *Charlie and the Chocolate Factory*. Her penultimate song, "I Want It Now," right before she vanishes down a 'bad egg' tube, is the quintessential representation of SSBS. That's *Selfish Spoiled Brat Syndrome*, for the layman.

I love the episode from *Malcolm in the Middle* where parents Lois and Hal go to the water park with their sons Malcolm and Reese. The boys act like spoiled brats and attempt to one-up each other through retaliation the entire time, wrecking the nice day that the parents had planned. Finally, after one such retaliation, Reese chases Malcolm up a water slide stairway after splashing a newly-purchased soft drink all over Hal's shirt. Hal is fazed, and Lois is, well, Lois is another angry adverb.

Lois pursues them up the slide, standing in front of them at the apex of a giant water slide as they stand there being scolded. The script goes like this:

Lois: *Do you think we're wealthy?! Wealthy people drive fancy cars. They have fresh pasta. Do we do any of those* *things?! NO! Wealthy people can afford any of their vacations ruined, no big deal. They just pick up and go again. Your father and I worked so hard, so long. What is wrong with you two?! Are you aborigines?! Every time I turn around, I hear someone screaming and fighting. And I pray to God that's someone else's children, but it's not, it's always you! Sane children would appreciate this. Are you even thinking? No, you're always at each other like a couple of rabid monkeys. It is not enough you two do this every day, but you have to make me suffer. Well, so help me.... [She comes to the realization that Reese and Malcolm are up to something since they are looking back and forth at each other while she's scolding them.]*

Lois: Don't you dare!

[Malcolm pushes Lois down the slide by the finger and she screams, falling in backward with a diminishing wail.]

Attendant: *Arms and legs crossed at all times!*

Reese, looking in: *That's the bravest thing I've ever seen you do.*

Malcolm: *Yeah.*

Reese: *You're gonna die.*

Malcolm: *I know. So, you think she's gonna be okay?*[19]

And, like any good revenge story, Lois was there all the time, just inside the water slide entrance. Her hand reaches in and grabs Malcolm by his nose-plug necklace and Reese by the arm, pulling them in with a fierce growl as they all go plummeting down the slide.

What Malcolm and Reese needed was to obey. Since they didn't, they needed a scolding and butt-kicking by Lois.

What's the point, Aaron? Though I am known for endearing rabbit trails (ask any of my former voiceover blog readers or for that matter anyone in my immediate friend/family circle) I assure you there is one.

The point is that, ultimately, the boys didn't appreciate the gift that they had been given of a day at the waterpark. Poor little brother Dewey was stranded at home with an ear infection. Malcolm & Reese weren't. Yet they chose to squander their day through retribution and mayhem, in turn wrecking the veritable peace and relaxation Hal and Lois were hoping to obtain. And I *love* that Lois gets them back after Malcolm pushes her down the slide.

Oh, and the other point? Moms always win. ☺

Finally, chew on this. God is not a gumball machine. You don't just put a quarter into a slot in God and expect any number of different colored gumballs to come rolling down the lane into your hand, providing instant chewing pleasure. He's not into dopamine hits. He's into **YOU** being a hit. And the only way He can do that is to dispense what you need; not what you want.

There is a vast chasm of difference between wants and needs. I'll return to that in a bit, but first, let's take a flight together.

Chapter 4: The God of Airplanes

"But God demonstrates his own love for us in this:
While we were still sinners, Christ died for us."

- Romans 5:8

When do many people finally believe in God?

I know the answer, pick me, pick me! And I think you know
it as well. We believe in Him when Christmas is
approaching. When bills are coming due. Or, when we're
about to set foot on that airplane.

Don't be so coy. You know it's true, and so do I. So many people suddenly believe in God once their plane is about to take off. And once it's safely landed again, barring any unforeseen incidents in the interim (which also prompt sudden, convenient, miraculous belief in God), they're done believing.

I don't know about you (actually, yes I do), but if you're anything like me, you pray for your flight. And do you know why you do that? Because the piloting of said flight is out of your hands.

How ironic: we hardly ever pray – if we do at all – when we set foot in our own cars, *because we are in charge.* We don't pray because we believe we know best, and we believe we can take care of ourselves better than God. Statistically speaking, airplanes are still the safest way to travel. Far less loss of life occurs per year in air travel than there does on roadways. We just tend to focus on the spectacle and the totality of air disasters because they're so dramatic and usually end in total loss of life, whereas automobile accidents can sometimes see lives spared.

People find God on a plane.

Anytime the control gets taken out of our hands, we desperately want it back. We plead for it back. And when we know we can't get it back, we pull the old tried and true "go straight to the top" move.

"Are you there, God? It's me, Margaret."

Atheists suddenly, conveniently, believe that there is a God who just might hear their prayers and graciously, benevolently ensure that their plane touches down where and how it should, and oh! on time, please, *thankyouverymuch.* With no thought to what God can do to you and for you in a tense journey in the interim, they fuss and freak out the moment they have to relinquish surrender of the helm.

Let me tell you something. Brett James, Hillary Lindsey and Gordie Sampson wrote Carrie Underwood's "Jesus Take The Wheel" for a reason:

That day started out to be a typical "day at the office": We wrote it at Hillary's house. We were trying to think of ideas, and Gordie walked in and said, "I have this title, and I don't know what to do with it: "When Jesus Takes the Wheel."" Hillary and I both laughed. I thought it was kind of silly, to be honest with you; I thought, "What in the world does that mean?"

We kind of talked about it a while, then went around with five or six other song titles to write something else. We couldn't think of anything else and went back to Gordie's idea. Sure enough, we started writing it about the girl driving on Christmas Eve with a baby in the backseat of her car. It evolved into "Jesus, Take the Wheel" soon after that.

My wife had a similar experience to the girl in the song: My wife had a car crash when we were dating. She nearly died. Her car spun around several times and went under an 18-wheeler. She said she saw angels come help her. She walked away with no injuries. I thought it was interesting that she had that same situation happen to her like the girl in the song.

It became such a neat song because it touches people. Those songs are really special.

That will always be one of the most special songs to me.[20]

The lyrics speak of a woman who was driving and hit a patch of black ice. The chorus is as follows:

Jesus, take the wheel, take it from my hands
'Cause I can't do this on my own
I'm letting go
So give me one more chance
And save me from this road I'm on
Jesus, take the wheel

Now, did the woman let go and expect Jesus to steer for her? Well, not exactly (although I'm sure He can Daytona with the best of them). But what *was* involved was a measure of trust and surrender that God was able to do immeasurably more than all she could ask or imagine or think (Ephesians 3:20). This verse is *so* pivotal to our understanding of who God is versus who Santa is. God is not just some celestial gift giver in the sky waiting to dole out toys once a year and make everything all better.

Nor is he a Jim-Carrey-Bruce-Almighty character beleaguered by all of our prayers and finally hitting the "Answer All" button with a 'yes.' **No.** God knows *precisely* what we *need*, and requires our surrender.

God already knows we want to take off safely, fly safely, and land safely. He already knows that. (Here's where I picture God hearing our requests for 'traveling mercies,' rolling his eyes and emitting a thundering *Ugggggghhhhhhhh....*) Psalm 139:4 attests to the fact that He already knows what we're going to pray even before a word is on our tongue.

Even more to the point, God wants us to not simply call him just when we need something. He wants *fellowship*. I love the article on josh.org[21] about God wanting us to pray to Him, and thus, to draw near to Him. He wants it always!

John Eldredge's excellent devotional book, *Knowing the Heart of God*, talks about this at length. My former Pastor Lee Bennett of Northwest Community Church constantly preached on the 'Fatherheart' of God. God *desires* us to be in constant fellowship with him. God *wants* to be with us. He loves us as a father!

God already knows what we want. What we, and those in our lives around us *need*, however, is sometimes drastically, tragically different. Here's where the story, and the clouds we fly in, grow dark. I know of friends who have lost children to suicide. To tragedy. I know of people who have lost their loved ones, their careers, their mobility. I knew of a friend who got her life back through a knee surgery, only to lose it a week later to a fatal case of thrush.

Sometimes, God doesn't give us what we want. He instead gives us, and those around us, what we *need*. And what we and those around us need is salvation, drawing near to Him, and understanding the bigger picture. We don't always know what we need. We *think* we need money, and a sweet crib to hole up in. We *think* we need fame and power.

But what if instead of more money, we really need the one thing that is *so* hard to get: Time? What if *that's* what we

really need? Thinking of it from my children's perspective
– who thankfully at this point have no concept of money
and thus my wallet remains unassailed – all they want from
me is my time. They just want Daddy to play with them!
They want more time with him and want him to get off
work. Santa can't give them that! Only Father Time can.
They don't need money; they need more time. What an
innocent and beautiful perspective!

What if we *want* to go to that concert, but God knows that
the ceiling or floor is going to collapse and dozens will
die…but he *needs* us alive?

What if we *want* to go into global ministry, but we *need* to
stay right here in the world and shine His light to
neighbors?

What if we *want* to get a dog because we love dogs, but
we *need* to protect our newborn baby and that dog might
not be safe with it?

What if we *want* to go to college in Boston, but God has
our future spouse in Seattle and we *need* to be close to
them?

What if we *want* to bring in a refugee family into our home,
but we *need* to work on our marriage and our own family
first?

Sometimes, despite our best prayers, our most fantastic orations and our most well-worded petitions, God knows that we need something else. Even beyond that, He wants us to love and worship him not just for the answered prayers, and not just in circumstances of duress or desire. He wants us to draw near to Him, and He will draw near to us. (James 4:8).

He doesn't just want airplane prayers. He wants <u>us</u>.

I daresay that He *needs* us, which is a great segue to the next chapter.

Let's talk about wants vs. needs now.

Chapter 5: Wants vs. Needs

"What I like and what I need's two different things."

\- JD Jordan in *Calamity: Being an Account of Calamity Jane and Her Gunslinging Green Man*

For me, I desperately *wanted* a newer house in 2020 when we moved in the middle of a pandemic. One with bullnose corners and high ceilings, and was modern, spacious, and beautiful. A 'dream home,' if you will. We found one! I thought we were going to get it! However, God said, 'nope.'

Instead, we 'settled' on a house in an entirely different neighborhood in Olympia, Washington.....and I thank God forever for it. It is most certainly *not* the house that I *wanted,* and not the one that I would have chosen. It's older, it doesn't have the high ceilings (except, kind of…in places)… but it has **so** much charm to it. And, being an older house, it has good bones. It definitely has the space to boot: over 4000 square feet on 3.88 acres.

But that's all window dressing. Why did we *need* to move there? My old best friend lives right across the street. I had never met him, but God had. And God knew I *needed* Roland at the time.

And his wife, *Rachel?* God knew that my wife Janine *needed* Rachel as her best friend at the time.

And their son, Oliver? God knew that my son, Brennan – the exact same age as Oliver – *needed* him.

And their daughter, Anya? God knew that my son, Asher – a year younger than her – *needed* Anya. (They're *adorable* together; I've already designed their wedding invitation. I am not kidding. It's all arranged.)

The point being, we each had a person! God *meant* for us to be there! My original best friend, my cousin and I, have drifted apart, and though he was my best friend at one point, God brought a surrogate in – as he has often done in my life – and provided me Roland when I needed him.

Beyond that, we absolutely LOVE where we live; the boys love their school; we love our property…we were *meant* to be here.

My eldest son Brennan is known to ask repeatedly for a Dr. Pepper if he knows that they're anywhere on the premises. I swear that kid has a sugar-detecting gene in his DNA, because if there's sucrose *anywhere* nearby, he's like a little fruit bug or a sugar ant. He WILL find it. He had a problem with bedwetting at one point, and would request soda near bedtime; it was absolutely out of the question, because we knew what would happen if we gave it to him.

He can pursue sugar so much that it affects his emotions when he doesn't get it, and he can glower and sulk like the best of them. He may have just come off one of the greatest experiences in his life, akin to winning Publisher's Clearinghouse for kiddos….but the moment he doesn't get that Dr. Pepper, that 12 ounces of happiness? Oh boy. Here comes the waterworks and his pint-sized fury. He forgets how good he has it, and focuses only on his frustration.

We're all trying to thread our way through this life and do the very best that we can with the limited knowledge we

have. We can only see twenty feet in front and behind us
if we're lucky. God, however, sees things on an *arc*, all the
way back to the beginning, and all the way to the end.
With his limitless vision, He knows what we truly need.

Sometimes, on that journey, I can be very guilty of claiming
that I know His will for me; claiming that I know what I
need, when truly, it's only a want. I elevate my desires to
the point of *necessities*, when, all along, they've needed to
stay in the small compartment that they were initially in:
desires. Necessities are rarely ever things. I don't *want*
air; I *need* it. I don't *want* health; I *need* it. I don't *want* the
shiny new iPhone; I *need* it, or I will die.

I am of course joking. I don't *need* that iPhone. But I do
have a strange tendency to nudge things that I want over
into the 'need' column far too easily. Sometimes I'll even
call it 'God's will for me.' (Just FYI, iPhones *are* in the
future for my boys, and they are my will for them. After all,
Android is not allowed or they will be permanently
banished.)

It's all too easy to erroneously elevate desires to necessities.

Figuring out the future, or even daring to claim that we
'know God's will' can be very, very dangerous. This is one

of the cruxes of my "The End" Christian dystopian series for the young protagonist, Sage Maddox. He thinks he is doing God's will and moves into a position to do so…but as such, has chosen a path fraught with danger to himself and others. How many times have we done that to ourselves?

We can only see so far into the future. *Our need sometimes lies well beyond our vision.* In fact, I daresay that it always does. We don't know what we need, so we operate on our want and call it our need.

We put things in the wrong columns all the time. We act out of justice and call it nobility.

We spend out of entitlement and call it comfort.

We retreat out of fear and call it self-preservation.

We are inclined to call things the wrong things.

My kids think they *need* Roblox. It is my great joy (and irritation) to continually remind them that they *want* Roblox. But at the same time, I *need* to protect them from strangers out there who infiltrate such innocent playgrounds to prey on the young. They are out there. My kids don't know this, and I don't necessarily *want* them to know this, but they *need* to know that I have two ultimate responsibilities with them. One is to provide for them, and the other is to protect them.

If providing something for them puts them in danger, then I haven't done 50% of my job.

God is the exact same way. It is His delight to provide for us and ensure that we have what we need. (Jeremiah 29:11). However, it is also His desire to protect us (Psalm 91). One should not cancel out the other.

If by providing for my children I've endangered them, I haven't done my job.

So, I ask you: should God be any different? So many people in the world today are conditioned to pray for deliverance from their pain. We can't stand it, and we want out of it right away. We'll do anything in the name of conflict avoidance. We try to pray it away, a la "God, please deliver us from this."

But what if 'this' is *precisely* what you need to go through? What if you don't *want* to go through it, but you *need* to? Santa would deliver you two tickets to the Bahamas for a month in order for you to forget your pain and get some R&R under the sun. But is that really the solution?

What if I posited that you might grow even *stronger* as a Christian, as a person, as a *human*, if you went through the very thing that you are now praying you don't have to go through? What doesn't kill us makes us stronger, right?

I have gone through some pretty heinous things in my life. Things I would never wish on anyone. And in many cases, I had to learn the hard way. Some people do. My 9-year-old is the same way. Headstrong people always have to learn the hard way. We want it *our* way; the Veruca Salt way; the no-pain way. But what if pain is truly God's megaphone to rouse a deaf world, as C.S. Lewis famously wrote?[22]

One of the reasons I so love Alanis Morissette as a lyricist is that the lyrics she writes are incredibly poignant and revealing; honest and insightful. They're challenging. One of my favorite songs of hers comes from the album *So-Called Chaos.* It's called "Out is Through." Here are the lyrics:

Every time you raise your voice, I see the greener grass
Every time you run for cover, I see this pasture
Every time we're in a funk, I picture a different choice
Anytime we're in a rut, this distant grandeur

My tendency to want to do away feels natural and
My urgency to dream of softer places feels
understandable, but I know

The only way out is through, The faster we're in, the better
The only way out is through ultimately
The only way out is through, The only way we'll feel better
The only way out is through ultimately

Every time that I'm confused, I think there must be easier
ways
Every time our horns are locked I'm towel throwing
Every time we're at a loss, we've bolted from difficulty
Anytime we're in stalemate, a final bowing

My tendency to want to hide away feels easier and
The immediacy is picturing another place comforting to go

The only way out is through, The faster we're in, the better
The only way out is through ultimately
The only way out is through, The only way we'll feel better
The only way out is through ultimately

We could just walk away and hide our heads in the sand
We could just call it quits, only to start all over again
With somebody else

*Every time we're stuck in struggle, I'm down for the count
that day
Every time I dream of quick fix, I'm assuaged
Now I know it's hard when it's through and I'm damned if I
don't know a quick fix way
What formerly was treatment, silence, now outdated*

*My tendency to want to run feels unnatural now
The urgency to want to give to you what I want most feels
good, and I know*

*The only way out is through, The faster we're in, the better
The only way out is through ultimately
The only way out is through, The only way we'll feel better
The only way out is through ultimately
The only way out is through, The faster we're in, the better
The only way out is through ultimately
The only way out is through, The only way we'll get better
The only way out is through ultimately[23]*

I think the most poignant lyrics in this song are right here:
*"Every time that I'm confused, I think there must be easier
ways. Every time our horns are locked I'm towel throwing.
Every time we're at a loss, we've bolted from difficulty.
Anytime we're in stalemate, a final bowing."*

Isn't that so human nature, to run at the first sign of
conflict? We are so risk-averse, us frail humans. Our

desire is to avoid pain. But I submit to you, Rocky said it best in the movie Rocky Balboa:

"The world ain't all sunshine and rainbows. It is a very mean and nasty place and it will beat you to your knees and keep you there permanently if you let it. You, me, or nobody is gonna hit as hard as life. But it ain't how hard you hit; it's about how hard you can get hit, and keep moving forward. How much you can take, and keep moving forward. That's how winning is done. Now, if you know what you're worth, then go out and get what you're worth. But you gotta be willing to take the hit, and not pointing fingers saying you ain't where you are because of him, or her, or anybody. Cowards do that and that ain't you. You're better than that!"

It ain't how hard you hit; it's about how hard you can get hit, and keep moving forward. How much you can take, and keep moving forward.

SO INSPIRING! We want to hit at life: to be a success, to make our mark, to impress and wow, to amass and acquire, to achieve and conquer, and to leave our legacy. But what we *need* to do is to get hit, and yet keep moving forward.

That's how winning is done.

Here's a great article I'd like to share with you on Loving God When You Don't Get What You Want.[24] I found it to very insightful. The link is in the bibliography at the end.

I propose that we call a spade a spade, a want a *want,* and a need a *need.*

Chapter 6: The Dreaded Prayer List

"I pray because I can't help myself. I pray because I'm helpless. I pray because the need flows out of me all the time, waking and sleeping. It doesn't change God. It changes me."

- C.S. Lewis

I use the Prayer NB[25] app on my iPhone. I've used it for years. I find it's very helpful – AND it helps me observe a great track record of God's faithfulness, having answered so many of my prayer requests over time. I love it!

And I also hate it.

Don't get me wrong – it has its uses, and they are many. It's one of the more well-designed prayer journal apps I've ever seen, and I'm used to it by now. What vexes me with it, however, is how addicted to it I've become; how formulaic my approach to the Lord has become with a prayer app in mind, sweeping me through my prayer time.

How much I've treated God like he was Santa Claus.

In fact, just speaking honestly and candidly here, that particular app has been one of the primary reasons for my writing this book. Don't get me wrong, it *is* a great help to always know what to pray for. That is indisputable! It is wonderful to be able to keep my finger on the pulse of God working in my life. That is irrefutable.

But the major drawback from the Prayer NB app is that I've treated my prayer list as a Wish List. A Wish List for a God whom I still think should act much like Santa Claus.

So many years have passed since that little boy (me) flipped longingly through the Sears Catalog just waiting for beloved and coveted items to jump out at me. Yet here I am, almost 52 years old, and I'm *still* seeking Santa.

Instead of seeking God, I'm seeking Santa. I'm seeking prayers to be answered. It's like one of my favorite T-Shirts says: "Am I perfect? No. But - am I trying to be a better person? Also no."

I'm still seeking the gifts, not the Giver.

Now, I grant you, I'm not that vain nor narcissistic, although I do occasionally whine if my hair isn't perfect. Do I have some noble prayers on my list? Yes. Do I have prayer concerns on there for others, and not just for myself or my family? Absolutely. Are there good and perfect things that I'm reflecting on and praying for (Philippians 4:8)? Without question.

Ultimately, however, I have to say that, while all of those prayer requests are important to be sure, I err on the side of simply checking off the list each day, instead of immersing myself in the presence of **The Creator of the Universe.**

Again, I'm seeking the gifts, not the Giver.

Do I truly believe that God cares for me and my family? Yes. So, I shouldn't have to pray for that so routinely. All the hairs on my and my family's heads are all numbered

(Matthew 10:30). He knows what we need before we ask Him (Matthew 6:8). He truly does!

What we truly need, every single day, is like the old hymnary[26] sang:

> *Day by day, dear Lord,*
> *of thee three things I pray;*
> *to see thee more clearly,*
> *to love thee more dearly,*
> *to follow thee more nearly,*
> *day by day.*

Pursuing answered prayer from God isn't the same as pursuing God.

It just isn't. Pursuing *God* is pursuing God. And nothing less, as it should be.

King David requested deliverance from dangers and persecutions in approximately 18 psalms that bear his name.[27] However, David is credited with writing **73** of the 150 psalms in the Bible![28] Let me check my math. Yep, that's right, 44 are *not* about deliverance. Clearly, he was focused on more than just requesting deliverance from

Saul or other dangers. He praised His God, His King! He worshipped Him!

What we can get so stuck in is treating God like Santa. God is NOT Santa. He is the ultimate Gift Giver. He doesn't ride a red sleigh through the sky only one night per year, only delivering presents to children, and only if they're good. He is not limited to the North Pole, nor does He rear His head solely on Christmas Eve. He doesn't surround Himself with elves who do His bidding.

God is NOT Santa.

James 1:17 says, "Every good and perfect gift is from above, coming down from the Father of the heavenly lights, who does not change like shifting shadows." That means that you're not in jeopardy of being put on some 'Naughty List' and missing out on presents that year. (We're all on the Naughty List anyway, come on now. Especially that guy who just cut me off in traffic.) That means that God knows how to give good gifts to His children, and that He does not flicker or adjust who He is based on our behavior. It means that He is the Unchanging God, and just like His Son (who is God Himself), He "is the same yesterday, and today, and forever" (Hebrews 13:8).

With that in mind, I don't need to approach Him as such. He is not Kris Kringle, Jolly Old St. Nicholas, Sinterklaas, Father Christmas, Weihnachtsmann, Pere Noel, Saint Nick, Kanakaloka, Noel Baba, or any of the names numerous cultures have ascribed to Him.

No. He is Abba Father. Adonai. The Beginning and the End. Alpha and Omega. The Ancient of Days. The Anointed One. The Living God. El Shaddai. Immanuel. Jehovah. Yawheh.

deletes Prayer NB app to prove a point
reinstalls it again because he thinks he needs it still

We're still on that journey of figuring out how to properly pray. I think we always will be (Php 1:6).

Now that we know who God is *not*, let's talk about who He actually is.

Chapter 7: God is Not Santa

"For a time, I believed not in God nor Santa Claus, but in mermaids."

- BrainyQuote

I want to share with you one of the funniest things I have ever laid eyes on. Around the mid-90's, many urban legends and funnies were circulating the nascent Internet, and while working at my old church as an executive assistant, I came upon many of them.

One of them, in particular, caught my eye. Back then it was called "A Scientific Inquiry Into Santa Claus." Now, as I search for it, I find it entitled "The Physics of Santa Claus." It's originally attributed to Rod Morgan, Systems and Integration Office IRM/OPS/SIO, US Department of State, from an email he sent in 1987.[29]

To start off on discovering who God is, this should first give you a clue into who *Santa* is.

On or around Christmas, Santa delivers presents to all the good children of the world. Like all claims, this needs to be rationally examined.

1. *No known species of reindeer can fly. BUT there are well over a million species of living organisms yet to be classified, and while most of these are insects and germs, this does not COMPLETELY rule out flying reindeer which only Santa has ever seen.*

2. *There are 2 billion children (persons under 18) in the world. BUT since Santa doesn't (appear) to handle most Muslim, Hindu, and Buddhist children, that reduces the workload to 15% of the total - 378 million according to Population Reference Bureau. At an average (census) rate of 3.5 children per household, that's 91.8 million homes. One presumes there's at least one good child in each.*

3. *Santa has 31 hours of Christmas to work with, thanks to the different time zones and the rotation of the earth, assuming he travels east to west (which seems logical). This works out to 822.6 visits per second. This is to say that for each Christian household with good children, Santa has 1/1000th of a second to park, hop out of the sleigh, jump down the chimney, fill the stockings, distribute the remaining presents under the tree, eat whatever snacks have been left, get back up the chimney, get back into the sleigh and move on to the next house. Assuming that each of these 91.8 million stops are evenly distributed around the earth (which, of course, we know to be false but for the purposes of our calculations we will accept), we are now talking about .78 miles per household, a total trip of 75½ million miles, not counting stops to do what most of us must do at least once every 31 hours, plus feeding and etc. This means that Santa's sleigh is moving at 650 miles per second, 3,000 times the speed of sound. For purposes of comparison, the fastest man- made vehicle on earth, the Ulysses space probe, moves at a poky 27.4 miles per second - a conventional reindeer can run, tops, 15 miles per hour.*

4. *The payload on the sleigh adds another interesting element. Assuming that each child gets nothing more than a medium-sized Lego set (2 pounds), the sleigh is carrying 321,300 tons, not counting Santa, who is invariably described as overweight. On land,*

conventional reindeer can pull no more than 300 pounds. Even granting that "flying reindeer" (see point #1) could pull TEN TIMES the normal amount, we cannot do the job with eight, or even nine. We need 214,200 reindeer. This increases the payload - not even counting the weight of the sleigh - to 353,430 tons. Again, for comparison, this is four times the weight of the cruise ship Queen Elizabeth II.

5. *353,000 tons travelling at 650 miles per second creates enormous air resistance - this will heat the reindeer up in the same fashion as a spacecraft re-entering the earth's atmosphere. The lead pair of reindeer will absorb 14.3 QUINTILLION joules of energy. Per second. Each. In short, they will burst into flame almost instantaneously, exposing the reindeer behind them, and create deafening sonic booms in their wake. The entire reindeer team will be vaporized within 4.26 thousandths of a second. Santa, meanwhile, will be subjected to acceleration forces 17,500.06 times greater than gravity. A 250-pound Santa (which seems ludicrously slim) would be pinned to the back of his sleigh by 4,315,015 pounds of force.*

In conclusion ... if Santa ever DID deliver presents on Christmas Eve, he's dead now.

See? Dead. So now you know. As God Himself is not dead, we've clearly established that they're not the same person. Poor flattened Santa.

So, I ask you: *does that sound like the God we serve?*

Indeed, no. The God we serve is active and alive.

I've heard it said that GRACE stands for God's Riches at Christ's Expense. *That's* what He gives us. We get what we don't deserve (salvation, eternal life), and we don't get what we do (punishment). Jesus Himself bore our sins in His body on the tree (1 Peter 2:24) so that we would not have to face the punishment that we deserve. It is *utterly amazing* what Jesus did for us. All at the direction of the Hand of God. This was His great master plan all along.

Grace. YES!! Santa doesn't give grace. Santa gives temporary presents. Things. You can't put a price tag on Grace. Or on salvation. Or on eternal life. Santa can't give you any of those.

It has become far too easy in our current cancel culture to substitute God and Jesus for things that are far more palatable and far less threatening. We do it because we don't like to squirm. But Jesus didn't come to comfort the disturbed; He came to *disturb the comfortable*.

So what have we done in response? We've thrown God out and put the Easter Bunny in His place. We've thrown out Baby Jesus and put Santa in His place. We've given up celebrating All Hallows Eve where we celebrate the saints who have passed, and instead dress up as witches and demons and monsters. Yikes!

Is it any wonder that the letters in Santa's name can be so easily rearranged to a name far more nefarious, far more sinister, whose destiny is the lake of fire?

It's become far easier to play "Happy holidays, happy holidays, while the merry bells keep ringing, happy holidays to you…" than to play "Joy to the world, the Lord is come, let earth receive her king…"

We substitute the inflammatory and the controversial for the unthreatening and universally acceptable. This substitutionary process must just break the Fatherheart of God. He *so* wants to be with us, to love us, to commune with us, and to provide for us.

With Santa in particular, we took the very moment God entered human history in flesh and blood, and instead of the Giver (God, the One and Only), we substituted Him with a giver (Santa). One of many. God is not 'one of many.' He is The One And Only.

There are so many ways that God wants to give us the gifts that we truly need. He wants to do the following:

1. Take care of our physical needs (Philippians 4:19, Matthew 6:31-32, Psalm 145:15-16, Luke 12:24-26, Mark 6:1-14, Genesis 9:3)
2. Give Us Rest (Matthew 11:29-30, Psalm 23:2, Exodus 20:8-11)
3. Provide Direction (Proverbs 20:24, Ephesians 2:10)
4. Give Us Grace (2 Corinthians 9:8)
5. Show Us How to Escape Temptation (1 Corinthians 10:13)
6. Help Us When We're Hurting (Psalm 34:17-20, Psalm 46:1)
7. Save Us (John 14:6, John 3:16, Romans 10:9)
8. Give Us Peace (Philippians 4:7, Romans 5:1, Psalm 23:3, Philippians 1:6, Psalm 107:9)
9. Point Us To The Truth (2 Timothy 3:16, Psalm 119:105)

There are so many more verses than the ones that I just listed, and so much more that God wants to do for us and give us.

God is UTTERLY AMAZING AND INFINITELY ETERNAL. He is all-powerful, omniscient, omnipotent, and omnipresent. He is not limited or confined, and is unrestricted. You cannot box Him in or shut Him out. He will not be pigeonholed to a single day or a single manner of giving or a narrow sphere of influence or operation.

No. He is GOD. All amazing and utterly fantastic. In John 1:18, John says, "No one has ever seen God, but the one and only Son, who is himself God and is in closest relationship with the Father, has made him known." Hebrews 1:3 goes on to say that Jesus, The Son, "is the radiance of God's glory and the exact representation of his being, sustaining all things by his powerful word. After he had provided purification for sins, he sat down at the right hand of the Majesty in heaven."

WHOA. So, if we know Jesus, we know the Father?

Yep.

After all, the account of Jesus talking with Philip in John 14:9 says this: 'Jesus answered: "Don't you know me, Philip, even after I have been among you such a long time? *Anyone who has seen me has seen the Father.* How can you say, 'Show us the Father'? Don't you believe that I am in the Father, and that the Father is in me? The words I say to you I do not speak on my own authority. Rather, it is the Father, living in me, who is doing his work."

John 10:30, Jesus says, "I and the Father are one."

DOUBLE-WHOA! AMEN! Jesus IS the Father! The Father IS Jesus! And Jesus ain't no Santa.

So, I say we abandon the "Santa Claus is coming to town" mentality that we've all been so conditioned with, and instead adopt the song, daily, of "Come, Jesus, Come" by Cece Winans and Shirley Caesar:

Sometimes I fall to my knees and pray
Come, Jesus, come
Let today be the day
Sometimes I feel like I'm gonna break
But I'm holding on
To a hope that won't fade

Come, Jesus, come
We've been waiting so long
For the day You return
To heal every hurt and right every wrong
We need You right now
Come and turn this around
Deep down I know this world isn't home
Come, Jesus, come

There'll be no war

And there'll be no chains

When Jesus comes

Let today be the day

He'll come for the weak

And the strong just the same

And all will believe in the power of His name

Come, Jesus, come

We've been waiting so long

For the day You return

To heal every hurt and right every wrong

We need You right now

(Come and turn this around) turn this around

Deep down I know this world isn't home

Come, Jesus, come

Come, Jesus, come

One day He'll come

And we'll stand face to face

Come and lay it all down

'Cause it might be today

The time is right now

There's no need to wait

Your past will be washed by rivers of grace

Come, Jesus, come

We've been waiting so long

For the day You return

To heal every hurt and right every wrong

We need You right now

(Come and turn this around) turn this around

Deep down I know this world isn't home

Come, Jesus, come

Come, Jesus, come

Come, Jesus, come[30]

Maranatha, Lord. Come. May we expect you every single day, with every single fiber of our being. May we long for you, unquenchably, thirstily, hungrily, knowing there is absolutely nothing else that can possibly assuage our pain, calm our fears, make all right and restore everything… forever.

Come, Jesus, Come. God The Father, through your Son, In Jesus' Name, COME.

Chapter 8: God? Help!

"When you follow God's will for your life, you can see how yesterday's events prepared you for today's challenges and tomorrow's opportunities."

- David Jeremiah

So there I was, in the spring of 2023. My voiceover career had been constantly, slowly eroding under the weight of AI, the economy, the SAG-Aftra strike, underbidding colleagues, lowballing clients, and I had just left the very toxic online voiceover community.

I knew that I needed to do something.

The voiceover industry has had it pretty darn good up until now. It's a very lucrative business – or at least it was. For many years I was exponentially increasing our annual income, and having a blast doing it. I was a voiceover coach, and a blogger who eventually went on to write 300 very satirical voiceover blogs a la Dave Barry. I also went on to write and publish 6 successful voiceover books.

But something was happening. There was a sea change in the air.

Let me take you back to a few years before that, however.

It was the year 2017. I was a wedding videographer – which is Latin for *one who enjoys eternal torment* – and I knew that something else was on the horizon. I was open to it. Voiceovers were calling my name in a brand new and fresh way that they never had before. I had always done them in the background as a sort of 'add-on' to commercial videography, but ultimately never as a stand-alone service.

Well, I jumped with both feet (and my larynx) into voiceovers, and it paid off handsomely. It paid our mortgage, bought our vehicles, and put a lot of money into savings. I'm very grateful! Over time, however, I began to witness a slow erosion that saw the income drop, the quality and quantity of available jobs drop, and with it, my sense of career stability.

So, jumping back forward to 2023, there I was, having just left the online voiceover community due to a large measure of toxicity present therein. I felt suddenly very isolated and immediately cut off in an industry that appeared to be flailing. I remember sitting there and asking myself, "what am I supposed to do?"

And then I just shut up and listened. No pleas, or begs or petitions to rescue me. I simply asked the question, and then I was quiet, waiting for the Lord to provide direction and guidance. Mind you, He didn't answer me with a James Earl Jones-esque voice or anything laden with trumpets, but I felt one thing for certain. It was a single phrase, echoing through my mind and my heart, convicting me of its truth. What was that phrase?

I'm a creator. I need to create.

And so, I jumped out of my seat, threw my hands up in resignation and full acceptance of this truth, and decided, that was it. I needed to create! It was really that simple. I felt such peace with this declaration, and such joy at the prospect. I've always been a creator; I've been able to create a living *being* a creator. And let me tell you something, having the gift of creation endowed to me by The Creator? WHOA. I don't take that lightly. I'm very, VERY grateful for it.

What followed leaving the voiceover community after having tried for so long to make inroads into the upper echelons (effectively beating my head against the wall in futility) saw me realizing a *bounty* of creativity.

In 2023, I created 2 musical albums (one of them entirely self-produced) and resurrected 4 previous ones. I had the time of my life in 2023 pursuing music again, both in studio and in live performances! I remain utterly grateful for those who took that journey with me: a journey that was thirty years in the making, since I officially started my music journey in 1993.

However, it was not to be. I *thought* that it was my calling to return to music. I was mistaken. (Here is where my wife grabs a tape recorder and asks me to repeat that I was wrong, just for the record.) It wasn't a calling to return to the *stage*, but it was a calling to return to *creation*. I had no idea that that 'creation call' was specifically for *storytelling.*

So, after yet another period of sitting and waiting on the Lord, I followed His leading into storytelling.

I am an author today because I faithfully answered God's call to be a storyteller. I love that I'm a parallel storyteller on two different tracks: one of them telling stories for my clients as a voiceover artist, and the other telling my own stories (I much prefer the latter). There are messages of faith, hope, resilience, trust, honor, and sacrifice in my stories – and there are even characters accepting Christ in there.

In November of 2023, I began writing the first few paragraphs of the *Dissonance* alien invasion trilogy. By November 20th, 2024, exactly one year later, I had published all *six* books in that series. But not only that: I had written and published a 9/11 historical fiction book called *Forecast*, a book of poetry called *Reflections*, a satire-slash-business reference guide called *The Superhero Anomaly,* a business guide to self-publishing, three children's picture books, and began working on my current project, a Christian dystopian trilogy entitled *The End.* I also personally recorded and produced 10 audiobooks of my works.

Talk about a fount of creativity!! In 2024 I sold 5500 books, and my *Dissonance* hexalogy all went bestseller status on Amazon and won several awards through Literary Titan, Reader's Favorite, and BookRaid. *The End: Alpha*, the opener, did the same. I'm so proud and grateful! And to top it all off, *Dissonance Volume I: Reality* has been adapted for the screen and is being pitched to streaming networks as we speak! Who knows what the status of that will be by the time this book is published?

I've been an author panelist at conventions, I've been a key reader and speaker at conferences, and I've enjoyed dozens and dozens of video interviews with podcasters talking about my books. How cool is that? All because of my calling.

All because I obeyed my calling.

All in all, I'm an author, and I LOVE being one. But I was one because I didn't whimper and plead with the Lord, asking Him to rescue my failing voiceover career, and to please 'make things happen.' I didn't tell him my hopes and fears and bring this list before Him of what I felt would fix everything according to my piddly little brain.

I'm an author, a creator, because I simply sat still and waited upon the Lord, listening for Him to direct me. I'm a creator because I love to create, yes, but it is what God wanted me to do.

I'll also say this, for the record. Voiceovers, though my career appears to be circling the drain, continue to support our lives *and* all the marketing I've invested into authoring and promoting my books. We have not been in want yet, and the cupboards have not been bare. He consistently provides, even if it's at the 11th hour.

God is faithful, and the Bible says that "God is not unjust; he will not forget your work and the love you have shown him as you have helped his people and continue to help them" (Hebrews 6:10). I am helping his people by authoring inspiring stories of love, faith, justice, hope, and trust. I am serving Him by scribing stories that testify to His presence and that lead people to Jesus, or at the very least, demonstrate characters being led to Jesus.

In December 2024, I was literally *called* again to write a Christian series. Though there is sparse profanity and intense situations in the *Dissonance* series as well as *Forecast,* as a Christian writer I had always struggled with that. I do desire verisimilitude, yes, and I want to paint a picture that contains a gritty dose of realism. We are not of the world, yes, but we are definitely still *in* it. To pretend that such language doesn't exist would be burying our proverbial heads in the proverbial sand.

So? I was called to write a series that had *NO* profanity in it. No sex, no drugs, no barbaric violence (though Dissonance had very little or none of any of those three things; just some sparse profanity) – I was to write *clean* fiction.

I didn't pray, "God, please give me an idea for a book series that will sell." I sensed in my spirit – strongly – that this is what He wanted me to do. Romans 8:26 says, "In the same way, the Spirit helps us in our weakness. We do not know what we ought to pray for, but the Spirit himself intercedes for us through wordless groans." I was convicted by the language that I had to employ in *Dissonance* to obtain that gritty dose of realism, and my spirit knew that.

As a result, *The End* was born. It's a series testifying to God's power in the face of a future antichrist, and I'm SO proud of how it turned out! As of this writing, the first book is out, the second is with the editor, and the third is coming along handsomely!

And then He called me to write this book, *God Is Not Santa,* because of the frustration I felt about how I was approaching Him in prayer.

God's gifts and His call are irrevocable.

That's straight out of Romans 11:29, and I believe it. All along, God had been calling me, and I believe that one day I will not be a voiceover artist who also does authoring.

I will be an *author* who also happens to do *voiceovers*.

Like Mary prayed, "I am the Lord's servant. May your word to me be fulfilled" (Luke 1:38).

AMEN! God knows, and God hears, and God calls. Even though I didn't come to Him with a list of "HELP ME!" prayers, He knew, and He heard, and He called me.

AMEN.

Chapter 9: Asher's Way

At that time Jesus said, "I praise you, Father, Lord of heaven and earth, because you have hidden these things from the wise and learned, and revealed them to little children."

- Matthew 11:25

Let me tell you something. When it comes to prayer, we adults and grown-ups who have amassed all this knowledge and obtained doctoral degrees and pursued higher callings and so-called enlightenment of the mind?

Rubbish.

We've got it all wrong! Would you like me to tell you who has it all right? Prepare to have your mind blown.

5-year-old Asher. That's who.

My son is a little spitfire, and is known for telling someone he loves them approximately 4,378 times a day. And that's with a nap in there somewhere. (Without a nap it's closer to 936,271 times a day.) He exudes love and cheerfulness. After all, his name literally means "happy and blessed."

Every night at bedtime, we'll be gathered in one of the boys' rooms, and we'll all go through our nightly prayers. Asher usually likes to beat Daddy to the prayer punch, and then giggles when Daddy gives him the angry "you beat me!" face. But then, Ash dives right into his methodical 5-year-old wisdom and presents the following rote prayer nearly every single night.

Dear Lord, I really love my mommy, and daddy, and brother. I really love Winny, and Macy, and my family and friends. And today was the best day ever. In Jesus' Name, Amen.

There is power in simplicity.

Did you catch his prayer? I mean, really? It's nearly the same every single night, but we don't care. It's loaded with simplicity, and there isn't a single request to be found in it. No pleas, no wish lists, no requests for toys or things, opportunities, recognition, acquisitions or accomplishments. He simply wants to exude thanks for a day well done.

That's it! I absolutely love Asher's heart in this because it reflects where I *wish* mine was. Asher's heart seems to always be there 24-7. My heart seems to always have a hard time even purchasing the ticket for the *journey* there.

What can we learn from this little guy?

It's okay to bring absolutely nothing to the Lord except praise and gratitude.

Remember 'attitude of gratitude?' Yep. That's Asher. After all, doesn't God already know what we need? Haven't we covered that already? Aren't you tired of that same old refrain? Is it taking just as long to get through your thick skull as it is mine?

We can learn a lot from Asher. He's young, but that won't stop him. 1 Timothy 4:12 says, "Don't let anyone look down on you because you are young, but set an example for the believers in speech, in conduct, in love, in faith and in purity." Asher does that, and he has conduct, love, faith and purity in spades.

Thank you, my son, for setting the tone and keeping the pace. Thank you for leading the way and showing us all how it's done.

Thank you for bringing nothing to the Lord except praise and gratitude. No Wish Lists. Just praise and gratitude.

Thank you, my son, for teaching me.

Chapter 10: Burn The Ships

(And The Wish Lists)

"There are far, far better things ahead than any we leave behind."

- C.S. Lewis

God detests our new moons and our appointed feasts. His soul hates them! They have become a burden to Him. He is weary of bearing them (Isaiah 1:14).

He goes on to say, "So when you spread out your hands in prayer, I will hide My eyes from you; Yes, even though you multiply prayers, I will not listen. Your hands are covered with blood. Wash yourselves, make yourselves clean; Remove the evil of your deeds from My sight. Cease to do evil, Learn to do good; Seek justice, Reprove the ruthless, Defend the orphan, Plead for the widow."

Psalm 51:17 says that "a broken and contrite heart you, God, will not despise." Amen! God seeks worshippers who will worship Him in spirit and truth (John 4:24). He wants us to draw near to Him without agenda, without ritual, without pre-ordained structure or demands. He simply...wants us. How rich and beautiful is that?!?!

Matthew 6:33 says "Seek ye first the kingdom of God, and all these things will be added unto you." Psalm 46:10 says, "Be still and know that I am God."

Are you getting it yet?

God wants us to draw near to Him as if He is NOT Santa. NOT a slot machine. NOT a lottery. NOT Publisher's Clearinghouse. NOT a goldmine. NOT some fount of blessing.

What if we just simply drew near to Him, in silent reverence, saying absolutely nothing? What if we so hungered for Him that we were willing to bring all our requests before Him, and yet utter *none* of them to Him?

Could we do that? Could we hold all these important requests that are SO close to our heart, and yet not mention even a single one? Could it be that God already knows what they are anyway?

As mentioned before, I got in the habit of going through the Prayer NB app and just ritualistically scrolling down it, checking off each prayer, one after the other, feeling like I was fulfilling some kind of daily obligation.

Our prayer life should not be mere obligation.

Here's what I did to banish the Wish Lists from my life.

One of my favorite ways to approach God is to come before Him in humility knowing that He created my mind and He knows what's in it. He already knows! So why should I need to recite my list, one thing after another, ticking off a checklist of prayer requests, as if I were even able to surprise Him?

I leave my phone behind. I leave my expectations behind. I leave my desires at the door. I calm myself with zero sounds. I happen to be a voiceover artist with a sound booth that is tremendously quiet inside, and it's amazingly tranquil. My phone, with its prayer app, does not enter with me. It remains outside to not trouble me or hamper my prayers.

I challenge myself to sit for five minutes and just meditate. Above me, the wall-mounted iMac displays a screensaver of dolphins swimming peacefully beneath the waves; whales making their annual migratory route in silence; eagles soaring on the breeze, feathers fluttering; cascading aerial shots over mountainous terrain. All of it: so incredibly peaceful, attesting to the grandeur of my Lord, the One who created the entire universe, and knows me all too well.

He already knows what I need. He already knows what I want to pray for.

I sit in Psalm 46:10 silence and listen for the still, small voice, letting Him roam freely in my brain and my soul and my heart and my spirit. I let Him in. That's key! *I let Him in.* To do His work. To seek out darkness and expose it, then purge it. To cleanse me. To pour His healing, geyser-springing crystal clear water down through the mossy and muck-covered grotto of my soul. To inhabit me. To speak to me.

And I listen. Palms up, I listen and receive.

And then, perhaps I'll go through A.C.T.S. – Adoration, Confession, Thanksgiving, and *then* Supplication, time permitting….instead of formulaically going down a memorized prayer list, or one prompted by my phone.

When all is (not) said and done, I wrap it up with basking in His presence once more. I sit in silence. After all, as John Bunyan said, "In prayer it is better to have a heart without words than words without a heart." You also can't talk while you're listening, and you can't listen while you talk.

There is no Wish List in silence. There is no Wish List in tranquility.

Furthermore, there are no expectations. I am filled with the knowledge and reassurance that God in Heaven already knows the burdens of my heart, the desires of my soul, and understands what I need before I ask Him (Matthew 6:8).

I burn the ships and leave everything behind, for God to take me on a journey there in that quiet space, just me and Him, Him and me.

It is SO good and it is so rich.

See, for too long I got into the habit of treating God like Santa Claus. Limiting Him. Trapping Him. Boxing Him in. Expecting and demanding things from Him. And then, sometimes, even getting mad at God and, look out now! – *railing* – at Him for not coming through. But who am I to talk back to God (Romans 9:20-21)? Does not God have the right to do what He wishes, and in His own time?

One of my very good friends, and an indispensable ally in my authoring, is named Vance. Vance is a brother in the Lord who has been so supportive of my pursuits, and he has been faithful to review all of my audiobooks to ensure they're free of errors. I SO appreciate him!

At one point I was becoming discouraged with my authoring pursuits and the results. Sales were down, reviews were down, and as I was counting on this to be my pivot, my next move, my evolution past being a voiceover artist and the thing I wanted to do for the rest of my life, I was angry with the Lord for not delivering and making this a success "by now." I mean, why was I not a success by now?

In short, *what was taking Him so long?!?!*

Here's the thing. God doesn't work on our timetable. God works on *God's* timetable. With the Lord a day is like a thousand years, and a thousand years are like a day (2 Peter 3:8). He works in His OWN time!

So, knowing that, Vance said something to me that was laden with gentility. Sugar-coated with cooing and using kid gloves. Tender. He said,

"Here's the thing, dude! You have no patience!"

Ouch....? Thankfully, he went on to elaborate and soften the blow a bit, but that was the truth! And the truth sometimes hurts. Wait – not *sometimes*. It *always* hurts. I don't have patience! I expect things to happen on a certain timetable, within a certain duration, and if they don't, then surely something is wrong....right? *Where are you, God? Waaaaaah waaaaaaaaah WAAAAAAAAAAAAAAHHHHHH!!!*

At 51, I'm still incredibly immature in the Lord.

I chewed on what Mean Old Vance said to me for a long while after that, and eventually I started answering his emails and texts again once I got over my bitterness at him for being such a Grumpy McMeanieFace.

It's true: I have no patience. Not even a little bit. I need to wait, to calm myself, to stop and smell the roses. To *breathe*. To just calm down and relax. When God does something, or even *whether* He'll do something, is not up to me.

To think that it's all up to me relegates God to Santa status all over again.

We project our demands onto Santa and expect him to deliver what we want, and we know it will happen at least one day per year.

But is God Santa? No. Hence, the title of this book. God does not operate only on December 24th, nor does He have to. He can operate – or not – on His own timetable. Remember the chapter on Wants vs. Needs? I get my panties in a bunch because, in all likelihood, I'm *wanting* something I don't *need*. I'm my 9 year old wanting Dr. Pepper at bedtime. I have that, and I'm going to wet the bed. Period.

So? Burn the ships with me. Don't treat God like Santa Claus with your prayer list of demands and expectations. Bask in His presence. Trust Him. Listen to Him. Don't do all the talking in prayer and think that suffices. You were given two ears and only one mouth for a reason. *Listen.*

It's not clear who said it, possibly Mark Twain or Abraham Lincoln, but the phrase goes, "Better to be closed-mouthed and thought a fool than to open your mouth and dispel all doubt."

In other words, CAN IT! Quiet your mouth. Quiet your soul. Listen. Prayer doesn't mean you come before God like you have an appointment with Him and you're going over an agenda that He knows nothing about. He knows *everything* about your agenda. You can't bring anything before Him and surprise the Creator of the Universe, the One who created you.

He is unsurprisable. I just coined that word. You heard it here first, folks.

Therefore, close thy mouth, engage thine ears, and listen.

That's how I burn the ships. That's how I don't treat God like Santa, because He isn't some one-time-a-year cameo God. He's Immanuel, God With Us, and He longs to have an ongoing relationship with us. With me. With you.

1 Thessalonians 5:16-18 says, "Rejoice always, pray continually, give thanks in all circumstances, for this is

God's will for you in Christ Jesus." The New Living Translation says: "Never stop praying". The English Standard Version says: "pray without ceasing".

Pray! In the words of MC Hammer, "We got to pray, just to make it today."

May you have gratitude always. May you become a giver, and learn how to receive all things from the Lord. May you never invoke His Name only before a flight, but rather call upon His Name and His Power always. May you understand the profound difference between wants and needs. May your prayer list go unspoken; keep track of God's faithfulness, certainly! But may your heart be without words rather than the contrary. May you heed His call. May you realize who He truly is, and who He truly is *not*. May you be like Asher.

And may you burn the ships as you bask in Him. May your daily prayer life become utterly powerful, utterly connective... and utterly devoid of requests. This does not mean in any way that you shouldn't bring the important things to God and plead with him.

After all, Job pleaded with God. Abraham pleaded with God. *Jesus* pleaded with God in the Garden of Gethsemane.

But they all did it with one understanding:

God is not Santa.

Sometimes He'll give you what you want, sometimes He'll give you what you need, but all the time, he WANTS you to NEED Him. That's what He truly desires for us. In the ultimate battle of wants vs. needs, that's the one that matters most. So, need Him. God bless you richly as you do.

Love,
Aaron Ryan

Afterword

It is my prayer that the lessons and urgings provided in this book will encourage you to take the time to appraise your life, and the things in it, and truly put things in perspective.

It's far too easy to grow enamored with all that we've acquired, and to put our trust, our sense of security, our self-worth and our own inherent value, into *that*. When, in reality, all of that can be taken from us in a heartbeat. Our very functionality as a human can be taken from us in a stroke, heart attack, or diabetes.

As an author, I place far too high a premium on acceptance. That acceptance is conveyed to me anytime someone buys one of my books or leaves me a positive review. Someone who joins my exclusive Facebook group or asks me to speak at their event. I place too much importance on these things, and I know it.

For your own life, ask yourself, what do you place your trust in? Who do you rely on? Are you able to transfer that reliance onto God, the Lover of Your Soul, who knows your needs before you ask Him? He is "able to do immeasurably more than all that we can ask or imagine or think, according to the power that is at work within us." (Ephesians 3:20).

He is ABLE.

May you realize that God is not to be called upon solely when we need something. May you realize that God is your Loving Father, and He wants to hold you.

With love,

Aaron Ryan

About the Author

Award-winning and bestselling author Aaron Ryan lives in Washington with his wife and two sons, along with Macy the dog, Winston the cat, and Merry & Pippin, the finches.

He is the author of the bestselling *Dissonance* 6-book alien invasion saga, the dystopian Christian fiction saga *The End*, the sci-fi thrillers *Forecast* and *The Slide*, the children's picture books *The Ring of Truth*, *The Sword of Joy* and *The Book of Power*, the business reference books

How to Successfully Self-Publish & Promote Your Self-Published Book and *The Superhero Anomaly*, 6 business books on voiceovers penned under his former stage name (Joshua Alexander), as well as a previous fictional novel, *The Omega Room.*

When he was in second grade, he was tasked with writing a creative assignment: a fictional book. And thus, *The Electric Boy* was born: a simple novella full of intrigue, fantasy, and 7-year-old wits that electrified Aaron's desire to write. From that point forward, Aaron evolved into a creative soul that desired to create.

He enjoys the arts, media, music, performing, poetry, and being a daddy. In his lifetime he has been an author, voiceover artist, wedding videographer, stage performer, musician, producer, rock/pop artist, executive assistant, service manager, paperboy, CSR, poet, tech support, worship leader, and more. The diversity of his life experiences gives him a unique approach to business, life, ministry, faith, and entertainment.

Aaron's favorite author by far is J.R.R. Tolkien, but he also enjoys Suzanne Collins, James S.A. Corey, Michael Crichton, Marie Lu, Madeleine L'Engle, John Grisham, Tom Clancy, C.S. Lewis, Stephen King and Dave Barry.

Aaron has always had a passion for storytelling. Visit his author website at www.authoraaronryan.com, the Dissonance post-apocalyptic alien invasion website at www.dissonancetheseries.com, or *The End* dystopian saga website at thisisnottheend.com.

If you liked this or any of Aaron's books, please visit the Amazon and Goodreads pages for the specific book(s) and leave a positive review. Once it shows up, please email the screenshot of it to me@authoraaronryan.com for a discount on your next book purchase from him! Thank you so much. Reviews really do help a ton!

Visit Aaron's website and sign up at the Blog:

Subscribe to Author Aaron Ryan

Follow Aaron and connect on Social Media:

Connect with Aaron

Feel free to check out the following links for further information on Aaron:

Subscribe to Aaron's blog for free giveaways, news and new releases at authoraaronryan.com/blog

Join the Author Aaron Ryan exclusive Facebook community at facebook.com/groups/authoraaronryan

Subscribe to Aaron's YouTube channel at youtube.com/@authoraaronryan

Visit Aaron's social media links to connect with him at dot.cards/authoraaronryan

Also by the Author

As Aaron Ryan:

1. *THE END: Alpha*
2. *THE END: Omicron*
3. *THE END: Omega*
4. *The Complete "THE END" Christian Dystopian Series*
5. *The Ring of Truth*
6. *The Sword of Joy*
7. *The Book of Power*
8. *The Christian Kids Values, Identity & Affirmation Series*

9. *Dissonance Volume I: Reality*

10. *Dissonance Volume II: Reckoning*

11. *Dissonance Volume III: Renegade*

12. *Dissonance Volume IV: Relentless*

13. *Dissonance Volume Zero: Revelation*

14. *Dissonance Volume Up: Rising*

15. *The Complete Dissonance Alien Invasion Saga*

16. *Forecast*

17. *The Slide*

18. *The Superhero Anomaly*

19. *How to Successfully Self-Publish & Promote Your Independent Book: A Self-Publishing & Business Marketing Guide For The Independent Author*

20. *Reflections: A Compilation of Journals and Poetry*

21. *The Omega Room (abandoned in the early 90's)*

22. *Autobiography (no longer available)*

23. *Glimmerings – works of poetry*

As his former stage name, Josh Alexander:

24. *Voiceovers: A Super Business, A Super Life*

25. *Voiceovers: A Super Fun Pursuit*

26. *Voiceovers: A Super Responsibility*

27. *Running a Successful Voiceover Business*

28. *How do I get started in Voiceovers?*

29. *Five T's to Triumph: The Secrets to Getting Cast in Voiceovers*

Bibliography

[1] www.snopes.com/fact-check/mother-bird-sacrifice/
[2] www.lifestream.org/the-hen-and-her-chicks/
[3] www.history.com/topics/21st-century/9-11-attacks
[4] www.jfklibrary.org/learn/about-jfk/jfk-in-history/november-22-1963-death-of-the-president
[5] www.nasa.gov/mission_pages/apollo/apollo11.html
[6] en.wikipedia.org/wiki/Space_Shuttle_Challenger_disaster
[7] www.reaganlibrary.gov/permanent-exhibits/assassination-attempt
[8] en.wikipedia.org/wiki/Death_of_Diana,_Princess_of_Wales
[9] en.wikipedia.org/wiki/September_11_attacks
[10] en.wikipedia.org/wiki/Death_of_Michael_Jackson
[11] en.wikipedia.org/wiki/Columbine_High_School_massacre
[12] en.wikipedia.org/wiki/Parkland_high_school_shooting
[13] en.wikipedia.org/wiki/Sandy_Hook_Elementary_School_shooting
[14] www.texastribune.org/series/uvalde-texas-school-shooting/
[15] www.cnn.com/interactive/2016/09/us/911-children-age-of-terror/
[16] en.wikipedia.org/wiki/Casualties_of_the_September_11_attacks

[17] theallendercenter.org/about/team/dan-allender/

[18] en.wikipedia.org/wiki/PASS_device

[19] www.quotes.net/show-quote/49543

[20] theboot.com/carrie-underwood-lyrics-2/

[21] www.josh.org/devotional-god-hears-prayer/

[22] www.amazon.com/Problem-Pain-C-S-Lewis/dp/0060652969

[23] www.youtube.com/watch?v=tE28ahYAOk8

[24] lifeovercoffee.com/loving-god-when-you-dont-get-what-you-want/?srsltid=AfmBOorFTvdxxebyUduG9gHab2LHZ_AtNh_gLydpU3aa
NCvSVpTls8x2

[25] apps.apple.com/us/app/prayer-notebook/id522373829

[26] hymnary.org/text/day_by_day_dear_lord

[27] bible-daily.org/2011/05/10/david%E2%80%99s-deliverance-and-david%E2%80%99s-psalms/

[28] columbiaunionadventists.org/content/fun-facts-about-psalms#:~:text=David%20wrote%20at%20least%2075,confirms%20he
%20wrote%20Psalm%2095.

[29] www.washingtonflyfishing.com/threads/nfr-if-santa-ever-did-exist-hes-dead-now.18267/

[30] www.youtube.com/watch?v=MdhDtTOfG9o

www.ingramcontent.com/pod-product-compliance
Lightning Source LLC
Chambersburg PA
CBHW031212270326
41931CB00006B/529